# TREES
## AND THEIR
## WORLD

By Carroll Lane Fenton
and
Dorothy Constance Pallas

Cover Illustration by Ecaterina Leascenco
Illustrated by Carroll Lane Fenton
Cover Design by Elle Staples
© 2019 Jenny Phillips
goodandbeautiful.com
First published in 1962

# TABLE OF CONTENTS

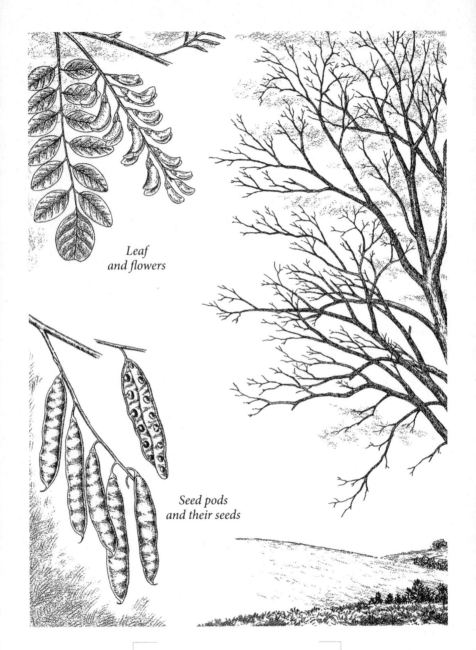

Leaf
and flowers

Seed pods
and their seeds

A black locust shows what trees are.

# TREES AND THEIR FAMILIES

A locust tree stood on a bare, snowy field. The tree had a straight trunk that grew upward 10 or 12 feet and then divided. The twigs and smallest branches looked smooth, but the bark on the trunk was thick and had cracked into coarse furrows and ridges. The furrows were reddish or yellowish brown, but the ridges were very dark. They showed why this kind of tree is known as the *black* locust.

Although the bark on the locust twigs was smooth, sharp spines grew out of it. The twigs also bore clusters of dark brown pods filled with orange-colored seeds. Wind often rattled the seed pods or scraped them against each other.

The black locust seemed to be dead, for it had no leaves. Really, it was only resting during the months of the winter. When spring came, the tree's roots would get water from the ground. Then the inner part of the bark would begin to make wood, and buds on the twigs would grow into leaves. Soon other buds would develop into flowers with a sweet, honey-like odor. Some of the people who smelled the flowers would call the tree a "honey" locust. That name, however, really belongs to trees with smaller leaves, longer pods, and clusters of forked spines that grow on large branches and the trunk.

The leaf buds of most trees are easily seen, for they grow outside the bark. But black locust buds are hidden in it and do not show till they swell in the spring. Leaves that grow from the buds are yellowish green. They are also compound, or made up of several parts. Each leaf has a central stem, with four to eight leaflets on each side and one more at the tip. The whole compound leaf becomes 8 to 16 inches long.

On sunny days the leaflets spread out on both sides of the stem, but they droop, or hang downward, when the sun disappears. We sometimes say the leaves "go to sleep" after sunset and on dull, rainy days.

Black locusts bloom when the leaves are almost grown. The flowers are about an inch long and look like white pea blossoms. They grow along stems that hang near the ends of twigs. Honey locust flowers are smaller and greenish. They also hang from places where leaves grow, not from the ends of twigs.

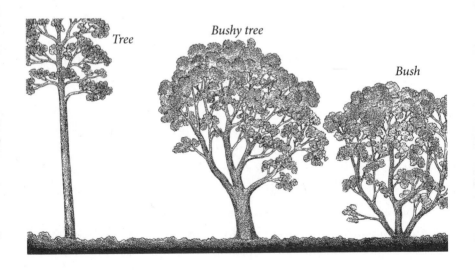

*Tree*

*Bushy tree*

*Bush*

*These drawings show a typical tree with its tall trunk, a bushy tree, and a bush or shrub.*

Black locusts grow wild on the Appalachian Mountains, from Pennsylvania to Georgia, and in a few other places. The homeland of honey locusts is much larger. It extends from Minnesota to central Louisiana, and from Virginia to central Kansas.

Black locusts have been planted in many places where they do not grow wild. People like their flowers and leaves, and pigs and cattle eat their seed pods. The roots form tangles that keep soil from washing away, and the trunks of young trees are cut into fence posts. The yellowish wood does not rot quickly in wet weather or when it is put into damp ground.

We use *plants* as a general name for weeds, grass, vines, and vegetables in gardens. The black locust is a plant, too, for it has leaves, stems, and seeds that grow into new trees.

Many seeds grow up, bloom, and die during one spring and summer. Others live almost two years, and many become much older than that. We call them *perennials*, or plants that live through the years.

All trees are perennials, for they have long lives. Trees also are *woody* perennials, for their trunks, branches, and twigs are hard. They can grow much larger and last much longer than stems that are pulpy and soft.

Bushes, which we often call shrubs, are also woody plants. So are long-lived, perennial vines. Many grapevines, for example, have woody stems three or four feet tall. Some grow taller than a man and are hundreds of years old.

We recognize vines because they climb or creep on the ground. But it is not so easy to tell a bush, or shrub, from a tree.

Some books say that bushes are less than 20 feet tall and have stems that branch out near the ground. None of the other stems are big enough to be called a trunk.

Trees are more than 20 feet tall, and they have trunks that do not divide near the ground. But some trees branch so much that they look bushy, and others may be either real trees or shrubs. The sassafras, for example, is a shrub on hills in northern New England, but it becomes a tree in the South. Some sassafras trees are 100 feet tall, and one that grew in New Jersey had a trunk almost five feet thick.

*Four members of the pine family. All are conifers, but the Western larch is not an evergreen, since it sheds its needles in the fall.*

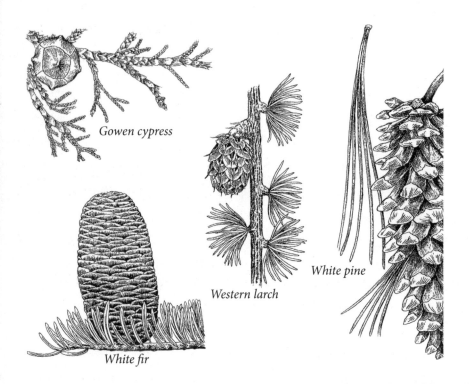

Gowen cypress

Western larch

White pine

White fir

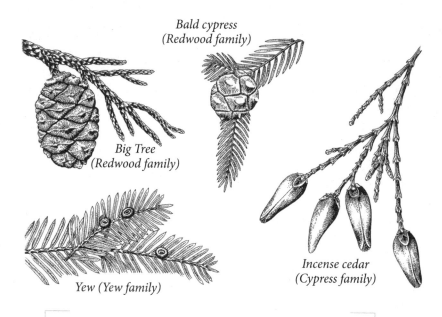

*Bald cypress*
*(Redwood family)*

*Big Tree*
*(Redwood family)*

*Yew (Yew family)*

*Incense cedar*
*(Cypress family)*

*These four trees belong to families which are related to pines.*

Trees belong to many kinds, or species, that have various sizes and shapes. Most fir and spruces, for example, grow so tall and straight that they look like green church steeples. Pines branch out and are not pointed at the top. Most elms resemble tall fans or vases, but California laurels are dome-shaped. Different species also have different leaves, as you can tell by looking at the trees in a park or woodland.

People who look alike are often related, or belong to one family. Trees belong to families, too, and their leaves, bark, flowers, and seeds tell us which kinds are related to which. Thus all pines have leaves so narrow that we call them needles, and their seeds are covered with cones. Pines plainly belong to one family, which also contains firs, spruces, hemlocks, and

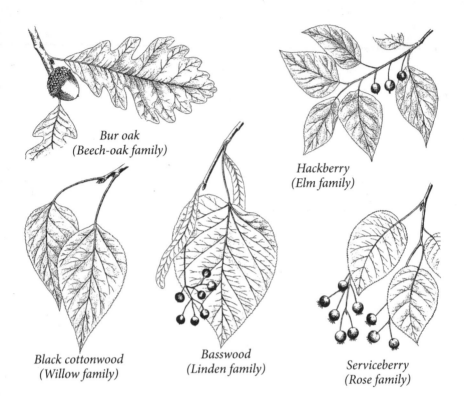

Bur oak
(Beech-oak family)

Hackberry
(Elm family)

Black cottonwood
(Willow family)

Basswood
(Linden family)

Serviceberry
(Rose family)

These broad-leafed trees belong to five different families.

tamaracks, or larches. These trees, in turn, are related to two
families made up of yews, redwoods, cypresses, cedars, and
junipers. We sometimes call all these trees evergreens, but
*conifers* (which means "cone bearers") is a better name.

We might think that all trees are related, since they are large
and woody. But that would be a mistake. Although conifers
belong together, their cones and narrow leaves show that they
are very different from locusts, oaks, and other trees whose
leaves are thin and broad. Even broad-leafed trees belong to

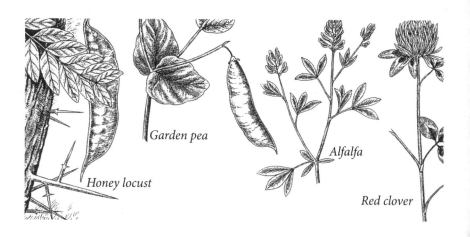

*Garden pea*

*Alfalfa*

*Honey locust*

*Red clover*

*These members of the pea, or legume, family are related to black locusts.*

different families. Oaks are not like locusts or maples, as we can tell by their seeds. Apple trees differ from elms, and basswoods are unlike hickories. Palms are still more different, for the veins in their leaves spread out from the stems instead of branching again and again. Palms are related to grass and lilies, but not to oaks, maples, or locusts.

Black locusts also have relatives that are much too small to be called trees. Locust leaves resemble pea leaves, the flowers look like pea blossoms, and the seeds and pods remind us of beans. We are not surprised to find that locusts belong to the family of peas and beans, or *legumes* (LEG-yoomz). This family also includes peanuts, clover, alfalfa, lupines, and wisteria vines, as well as acacias, palo verdes, and mesquite. Do you know any other plants that belong to this family?

# SAP AND WHAT IT BECOMES

"KEYOO, keyoo!" a sapsucker called as he flew through the woods. Soon he alighted on the trunk of a sugar maple.

The maple stood at the edge of a pasture. Its trunk, therefore, was not very tall, and its branches spread upward in all directions. If the tree had been in a thick forest, its trunk would have been tall and straight. Only a few branches would have spread out near the top.

The sugar maple's gray bark had cracked into strips or flakes. Leaves that grew on the twigs were *lobed,* or *cleft.* Both words mean that the outer part of each leaf was divided. This gave the leaf three or four pointed sections, or lobes, with "teeth" along their edges. All maple leaves are toothed, and some have many more teeth than there are on the leaves of sugar maples.

Sapsuckers are birds that belong to the woodpecker family. Most woodpeckers eat insects, which they dig out of bark or wood. Sapsuckers eat insects, too, but their favorite food is the sweet juice called sap, which they get from holes in trees.

This bird had been to the sugar maple before and had drilled many holes in its bark. Most of the holes were dry, but juice was oozing out of a few. The sapsucker perched near these holes and licked up the juice with his tongue. Then he hopped part way

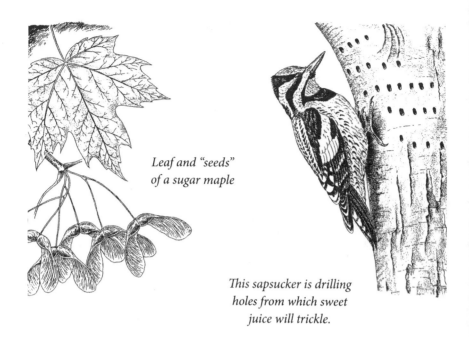

*Leaf and "seeds"
of a sugar maple*

*This sapsucker is drilling
holes from which sweet
juice will trickle.*

up the trunk and began to peck another hole.

As the bird pecked at the maple tree, his beak went through two layers of bark. The outer one was hard and dry, for the material in it had died. The inner layer was still living, and it was soft and juicy. The sapsucker ate some of this living bark and began to peck again.

Under the inner bark was a thin white layer which we call *cambium* (KAM-bi-um). This is where the maple tree grew, for the inner part of the cambium built wood, while the outer part made bark. The sapsucker swallowed some cambium and drove his beak deeper into the tree.

Under the cambium was a layer of sapwood. It contained thousands of tiny tubes filled with a liquid known as sap. It had come from the roots and was going upward to the branches and leaves.

In young trees, most of the trunk is sapwood. But the sugar maple was big and old, and sap tubes in the central part of the trunk had thickened and become hard. As they hardened, they became heartwood, which made the trunk stiff and strong.

The sapsucker did not peck into the heartwood. When his beak dug through the sapwood, liquid began to ooze into the hole. The bird licked up some of the sap and then flew away.

Some ants and a wasp came to drink at the holes when the sapsucker had gone. The wasp soon left, but the ants stayed too long. When the sapsucker came back, he found the hungry insects and ate them. The sugar maple was providing him with food as well as with something to drink!

Of course, the maple sap was not intended for birds and insects. Every tree has to have water and food in order to live. Sap contains both and takes them where they can be used.

Some small plants get water from rain or dew that falls upon their leaves and stems. But trees are much too large to do

*This piece from a log is magnified to show the parts that make up its wood and bark:*

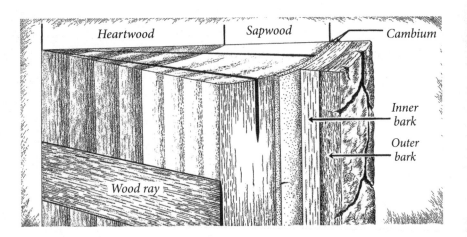

that. They have roots that grow into the ground and soak up water from the soil. The water also contains substances called minerals, which have been dissolved from the soil. They are some of the things which the plant uses for food.

If you could take a moving picture inside a living tree, you would see water come up into the roots. When it gets there, it becomes thin, watery sap. This liquid travels upward through tubes in the sapwood and finally comes to the leaves.

Leaves change the sap in two ways. First, they take out some of its water, which is used or evaporates into the air. Second, leaves produce sugary material which is the tree's principal food. Sugar dissolves in the sap, which flows out of the leaves and into the inner bark. The food-bearing sap goes through the bark till it reaches every part of the tree.

You know what happens when dissolved sugar and other foods are taken through our bodies. Part of the food is built into new flesh and bones as we grow, and part is used to mend structures that have begun to wear out. Some food is also stored away, to be used only if it is needed. The rest is changed by a process that is like burning, though it goes on so slowly that there is no smoke or flame. The slow-burned, or *oxidized*, food gives us energy to work, play games, read, and do all the other jobs that are part of living.

The same thing happens to food in sap. Part of it builds new wood, bark, and leaves, and part is used as energy. The rest is changed and is stored in sapwood and roots. When the tree needs extra food, this stored sugar goes back into the sap and is carried upward again. Maple sap is sweetest early in the spring, when sugar that has been stored in roots is taken upward to growing parts of the tree.

A large part of any tree's food is used by the cambium. Every

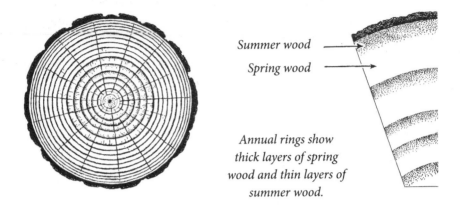

Summer wood

Spring wood

*Annual rings show
thick layers of spring
wood and thin layers of
summer wood.*

year it turns sugar into one new layer of sapwood and another
new layer of bark. Both layers take a lot of sugar, especially if
the tree is a big one. The cambium also slow-burns a great deal
of sugar to get energy for its work.

If you look at the cut end of a log, you will see circles in the
wood. These circles are often called growth rings. Since they
show how much wood the cambium made every year, they are
also called annual rings. You can tell the age of a tree when it
was cut by counting its annual growth rings.

Each growth ring has two parts, a thick one and a thin one.
The thick part was made in the spring, when the tree grew
rapidly. The thin part was made in the summer and fall. This
wood is fine-grained and shows that the tree grew slowly. If
both parts of the growth ring are thin, we know that the tree
grew slowly from early spring till winter. A cool season may
cause a thin growth ring. So will a dry season, or drought.
Leaves cannot make food when water is scarce or the weather
is cold. And when food is scarce, the cambium cannot make
much wood.

Trees of moist tropical countries can grow all year round,

and their rings are often hard to see. So are the rings of trees such as cottonwoods, which have soft wood and grow rapidly.

Aspen wood is weak and brittle, but most trees are strong. Cell walls thicken when sapwood turns into heartwood, making trunks and thick branches sturdy. Sapwood also contains tough fibers that make trees able to bend without breaking. Hickory wood, for example, is famous for its toughness.

As trees grow larger and thicker, their bark becomes very tight. The tight bark of a growing beech tree stretches, but in

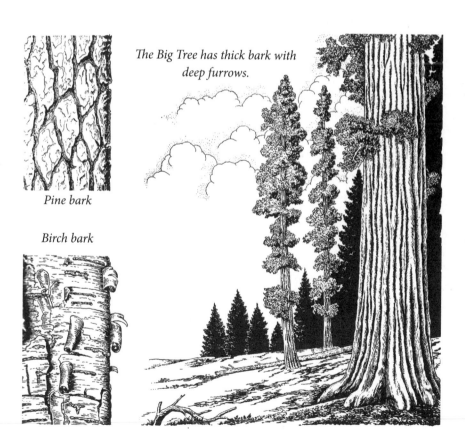

*The Big Tree has thick bark with deep furrows.*

*Pine bark*

*Birch bark*

time its outer layer splits and peels off. This uncovers newer bark that is stretchy—but in time becomes so tight that it also splits. Birches and madrones also have bark that stretches until it breaks and peels off. Madrone bark turns red and peels off every autumn. It exposes a smooth, greenish bark that is big enough to cover the tree.

Other trees have bark that is not stretchy and does not peel easily. Bark of this sort splits into strips or breaks into sections, which stay on the tree. This means that the bark becomes thicker and thicker while the cracks, or furrows, deepen. Black locusts have bark like this, and so do redwoods. Bark of the Big Tree, or giant sequoia, becomes as much as 2 feet thick, with furrows 18 inches wide.

Pines and hickories have bark that cracks and stays on the tree for a while but finally peels off. You will find piles of dead, peeled-off bark at the foot of many large pine trees. Hickory bark comes loose in strips that hang loosely until they fall. The long, rough pieces of bark give the hickory trees a shaggy appearance. In fact, one species is known as the shagbark hickory.

# LEAVES AND WHAT THEY DO

One spring morning a flock of red-winged blackbirds alighted on some black willows. The birds ruffled the red feathers on their wings and sang, "O-glee! O-glee!"

Some black willows grow more than 100 feet tall, but these were no more than 60. They seemed shorter than they were, for most of them had bent, stubby trunks that divided near the ground. Others had three or four taller trunks that grew up separately from the roots. These willows were shaped like bushes, though they were large enough to be trees.

Spring had hardly begun in March, but the black willows' buds were beginning to open. All the trees and bushes that belong to the willow family start to grow very early. The black flower buds of pussy willows often open while snow still covers the ground. At first we see only the silky catkins, but yellow flowers soon develop. They look fuzzy as they grow around the catkins.

The black willows would not bloom until late April or May, after their leaves had grown. They came from small red buds, in which tiny leaves had grown. Spring sunshine made the leaves grow and push against the red bud covers. At last the covers split and fell off, and the leaves began to unroll.

*The black willow has
narrow leaves and
two kinds of flowers.*

The new leaves were still small, and their color was greenish
yellow. But day by day, they became darker. Buds began to open
on other kinds of trees, too, though weeks went by before many
of them had as many leaves as the willows.

When the black willow leaves became full grown, they were
long and narrow, with slender tips. Small points and notches
along their edges looked like the teeth of a saw. All willow
leaves have saw-toothed edges, though some leaves are shorter
and wider than those of black willows.

We know that leaves make most of the food found in the sap
of trees. Suppose we look at the leaves of black willows again to
find out more about how this is done.

The first step in making food is for roots to get water from
the soil and send it through the trunk and branches. We say
the sap "begins to rise." Actually, trees contain sap all year
round. But more and more of it rises in the spring, even before
the leaves develop. When they unfold, the water they need is
ready for use.

The next step in food-making comes when air goes into the leaves. It enters through tiny mouth-like openings on the under surface. Every leaf can open these "mouths" or close them.

A leaf takes two things from the air that enters it: oxygen and carbon dioxide. Oxygen is used to slow-burn food and get energy. Carbon dioxide is the gas that makes pop and soda fizz. It is soaked up by *chlorophyll* (KLOE-ruh-fill), which is the material that makes leaves green. Chlorophyll also takes in energy that falls upon the leaves as sunlight. Using this energy, the green material combines carbon dioxide with water and then turns the combination into sugar. This process is called *photosynthesis* (fo-to-SIN-the-sis), which means "putting things together with light."

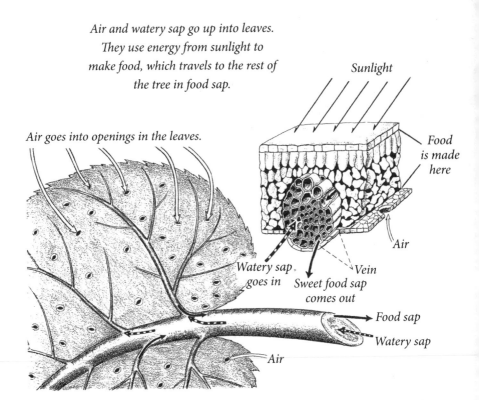

*Air and watery sap go up into leaves. They use energy from sunlight to make food, which travels to the rest of the tree in food sap.*

Sunlight

*Air goes into openings in the leaves.*

Food is made here

Watery sap goes in

Vein

Air

Sweet food sap comes out

Food sap

Watery sap

Air

Sugar made by leaves is not quite the same as the sugar we eat, and scientists give it different names. One type is called *sucrose*, and another is *glucose*. Sucrose is the sugar found in maple sap. Both types dissolve easily in sap and are taken to every part of a tree.

Did you ever wonder what happens after food is slow-burned, or oxidized? This process obtains energy but leaves waste materials, including carbon dioxide and water. In our bodies, these two substances are lost through the lungs and through tiny holes in the skin. Waste water forms the droplets that let you see your breath on cold winter days.

Trees need both carbon dioxide and water, but they cannot use the wastes left over when food is oxidized. They go out of the openings in the leaves, and carbon dioxide also is lost through the *lenticels*. These are spongy spots in the bark. You can see them plainly on wild cherries, birches, and many other trees.

Trees also lose water that evaporates from sap. This helps to cool the leaves, just as water that evaporates cools our faces and hands. But on hot, dry days, leaves evaporate more water than they can get from sap. When that happens, the leaves wilt or become limp. If leaves lose too much water and wilt too often, the whole tree may die.

Some desert trees keep from being killed by shedding their leaves during dry seasons. The palo verde (pah-lo-VAIR-deh), for example, has small leaves early in the spring and soon loses them. But the tree goes right on making food, for its bark contains chlorophyll. This explains the Spanish name, which means "green trunk" or "green tree."

When autumn comes, tiny sap tubes begin to close in the stems of black willow leaves. Soon a thin, dead layer forms

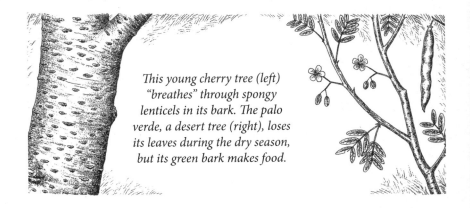

*This young cherry tree (left) "breathes" through spongy lenticels in its bark. The palo verde, a desert tree (right), loses its leaves during the dry season, but its green bark makes food.*

where each leaf stem is fastened to the twig. At the same time, chlorophyll dies, and other substances in the leaf change color. Willow leaves become yellow. Leaves of maples turn orange or bright red, and oak leaves become dark red or brown.

When all the sap tubes in a leaf stem are closed, the leaf comes loose and falls to the ground. All that is left is a scar on a twig, showing where the leaf once grew.

Many trees lose their leaves every fall, even where winters are not very cold. We call such trees *deciduous* (di-SIJ-yu-us). Other trees keep their leaves for several years. Some fall every year, but so many are left that the trees remain green. Most of these *evergreen* trees have cones and narrow leaves called needles.

The leaves of most deciduous trees are as wide as those of willows or much wider. Still, the holly is a broad-leafed tree that is evergreen, and so are the live oaks that grow in the South and the West. Tamaracks have cones but shed their leaves in the fall. We cannot call *all* cone trees evergreens or say that *all* broad-leafed kinds are deciduous.

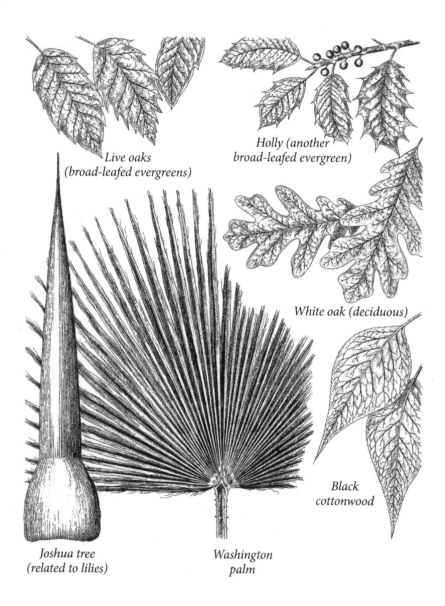

Live oaks
(broad-leafed evergreens)

Holly (another
broad-leafed evergreen)

White oak (deciduous)

Joshua tree
(related to lilies)

Washington
palm

Black
cottonwood

How veins are arranged in the leaves of various trees

Broad leaves have many shapes, but they are built on just a few plans. Some are simple, with only one flat part or blade. Other leaves are compound. They have several small blades, or leaflets, that spread out or grow on both sides of a stem.

Did you notice the ridges on a willow-leaf blade? We call them ribs or veins. They form a framework that holds the leaf in shape. They also are made up of tubes that take sap through the leaf.

Willow leaves have one main vein, or *midrib*, that runs lengthwise and divides the leaf into halves. Small veins branch off from each side of the main one and then divide again and again. But a maple leaf has several main veins that spread out like the fingers of your hand.

The leaves of date palms and coconut palms are compound. The veins in their leaflets run sideways, like the veins in a "blade" of grass. But fan palms and palmettoes have fan-shaped leaves with veins that spread out from the stem. So do veins of the maidenhair tree, or ginkgo. Ginkgoes ranged around the world during some ancient ages, but they now grow wild only in China. The ginkgoes you may see on lawns or in parks are cultivated trees.

# ROOTS, CELLS, AND GROWTH

A bald cypress grew in a southern swamp. The tree's trunk stood tall and straight, but it thickened and spread out at the bottom, rather like the "foot" of a vase.

The bald cypress had needle-shaped leaves and round, purplish cones, but it was not an evergreen. Its needles grew every spring but died and dropped from the twigs when fall came. In winter the tree was as bare as any willow or elm.

Many conifers live in dry places or even on mountaintops. The bald cypress cannot do that, for it needs a mild climate and a great deal of water. It grows best on low, damp ground or in swamps. Even when the swamps dry up, soil that covers the cypress roots remains moist.

Some trees have long, thick roots called *taproots* that grow deep into the ground. The roots of other trees spread out in a tangle near the surface. Roots of trees that grow in rocky places often twist and run along cracks.

Bald cypresses have no taproots, and they never grow in rocky places. Their roots spread out through the moist, soft soil and send cone-shaped humps up to the surface. These strange, woody humps are known as *cypress knees*.

Some people say that cypress knees resemble anchors which

Spanish "moss" grows on trees and
has almost no roots. It soaks up water
through its leaves and stems.

A bald cypress tree in
a southern swamp.
Spanish "moss" hangs
from branches, and knees
on the roots grow above
the water.

This picture
shows how
water comes
from spaces
between
grains of
soil and gets
into roots.

hold the trees to the ground. Extra roots do spread out from the underside of the knees. Those roots surely help to keep the trees from falling over when the wind blows very hard.

Other people say that cypress knees are used for breathing. We know that leaves, branches, and even trunks get air through openings and lenticels. Roots need air, too, and most of them get it from the ground. Even moist soil is loose enough to contain all the air a tree's roots need. But when water covers the ground, this air is pushed out, and the roots are threatened with drowning. Cypress knees grow above the water, however, and they are often hollow. Since the hollows are filled with air, they seem to help the cypress roots breathe.

Tree roots grow in various ways, but they all do the same jobs. They fasten the trees to the ground, they breathe, and they soak up water that contains dissolved minerals.

You can see how important the first job is by going outdoors after a bad windstorm. Trees with weak, damaged roots have been toppled over. So have many trees whose roots spread almost at the surface of the ground. But trees with taproots and roots that are large generally stand unharmed.

Breathing is important because it keeps roots alive. The whole tree will die unless most of its roots live and are able to get water and minerals from the soil.

We already know why water and minerals are important. You can prove that roots soak up these substances by sprouting a few beans on wet blotting paper. Do this in a dark place so the young plants will be white. Then put their roots into water mixed with red or blue ink. The colored water will soon show plainly as it goes up the white stems of your plants.

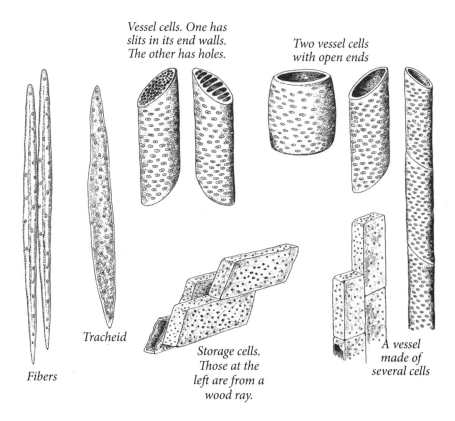

Vessel cells. One has
slits in its end walls.
The other has holes.

Two vessel cells
with open ends

Tracheid

Storage cells.
Those at the
left are from a
wood ray.

Fibers

A vessel
made of
several cells

Roots are also places to store waste materials and food. If
you dig up a piece of pine root, you will find that the heartwood
is full of pitch. This pitch is waste material which the tree has
stored in the root's dead heartwood.

We know that sugar maples store food in roots during the
summer. There it stays through the fall and winter. When spring
comes, the stored food goes into the sap and travels upward to
the twigs. Sapsuckers and insects eat some of this food. So do
people who gather the sap and turn it into maple syrup or sugar.
We use food which small plants have stored in roots when we
eat potatoes, carrots, or beets.

The water which most trees take into their roots is not found in puddles or streams. It is hidden away underground, where it covers grains of soil. This water makes the soil feel damp. It also makes a damp spot if you leave a handful of dirt upon a piece of rough paper.

Old roots are hard and thick, and they are covered with bark. Such roots hold trees in place, but they do not take water from the soil. That work is done by "feeder" roots, which are young and slender. The ends of feeder roots are covered with hairs, which soak up water just as a blotter soaks up ink. Root hairs also take in minerals, such as lime and iron, which the groundwater contains.

When sap goes from root hairs to leaves and back to roots, it travels through things called cells. Some cells are like tiny bits of jelly that have no special shape. The living portion of tree cells is jelly-like, too, but it soon covers itself with walls of stiff material. Such cells form roots, trunk, branches, and the other parts that make up a tree.

Wood cells die when they become fully grown, and their soft material disappears. This leaves only the stiff walls, which have various shapes and do different jobs.

Tracheids (TRAY-kee-idz) are found in pines, firs, and other conifers which have simple wood. The tracheids are stiff enough to make the wood strong but are so thin that sap cannot go through them as it travels up and down the tree.

Fiber cells are long cells with very thick walls and very small cavities. Sap can hardly travel through them, but they make wood stiff and strong.

Vessel cells are weak, for their walls are very thin. The vessel cells of the bald cypress and other conifers have ends pierced by holes or crosswise slits. Watery sap can move upward easily through such cells. Food sap comes downward through the same kind of cells in the inner bark.

Vessel cells in the sapwood of broad-leafed trees are open and look like tiny tiles. The cells fit together, end to end, forming long tubes in which sap flows upward from the roots. Food sap comes downward through the cells with perforated ends, which are found in the inner bark.

Some storage cells are long and slender, but others are short and wide. The slender cells are scattered among the fibers, but the wide ones are found in rays like those shown on page 25. Extra supplies of food can be stored in the cells that make up these rays.

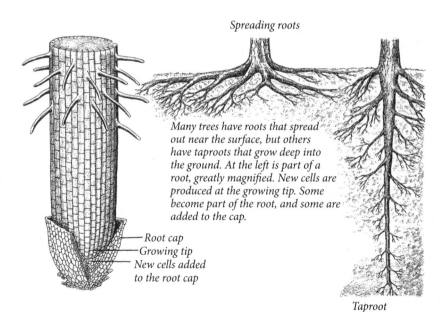

*Spreading roots*

Many trees have roots that spread out near the surface, but others have taproots that grow deep into the ground. At the left is part of a root, greatly magnified. New cells are produced at the growing tip. Some become part of the root, and some are added to the cap.

Root cap
Growing tip
New cells added
to the root cap

*Taproot*

We now are ready to tell how roots grow. The tip of each feeding root is made of living cells whose walls have not yet become hard. In the winter, these cells do not change, but when spring comes, they start to divide into halves. Each new half then grows into a full-sized cell.

Some of the new cells stay in the root, making it longer and thicker. Other new cells die and come off. They form a tough cap that covers the root tip and protects it from bits of sharp rock in the soil.

Cells divide, grow up, and divide again in every part of the tree. When this happens on the inside of the cambium, the dividing cells build new sapwood as well as new cambium. On the outer side, they build new inner bark, making it large enough to cover the growing wood. In other places, cells build up leaves and flowers. In time, cells that are part of the flowers divide and so build up seeds.

Most cells are too small to be seen except through a microscope. But millions of cells can form an annual ring of wood, and millions of millions can turn a sapling into a tall tree.

Cells can also push very hard when they expand and develop. Roots that grow into cracks often split huge rocks into pieces. Roots growing underground often break sidewalks and push the broken pieces upward. Such sidewalks are hard to walk on, but they show how much force cells can develop as roots become longer and thicker.

*Buds, flowers, and leaves of an apple tree*

# FROM POLLEN AND EGGS TO FRUIT

Small grayish white buds looked like fuzzy lumps on the twigs of an apple tree. The buds did not change during the winter, but when spring came, they started to grow. Soon their covers split open and fell to the ground.

Some buds contained young leaves, but others held both leaves and flowers. As many as eight leaves and seven pinkish white blossoms often grew from one bud.

The apple tree stood less than 30 feet high, and its trunk divided into many low branches. The twigs were thick and rough, and the flowers grew on especially short ones called spurs. The spurs of common apples are blunt, but those of wild crab apples may be as sharp as spines.

Both honeybees and flower flies came to the apple blossoms. The flies drank sweet juice, or nectar, which they found near the center of each flower. The bees drank nectar too, but they also gathered yellow, powdery pollen. They moistened the pollen in their mouths and then packed it into "baskets" formed by long hairs on their hind legs. When the baskets were full, the bees flew home. There the pollen was eaten by very young bees, or larvae, which were growing in the hive.

After several days the apple blossoms began to fall. Soon only their central portions were left—and these became larger and larger. In time they formed green apples that turned yellow or red as they ripened. When autumn came, the bright-colored fruit ripened and was ready to eat.

We have hurried from spring to fall in order to tell this story of buds, blossoms, and apples. Suppose we now go back to the spring, to find out what the flowers are made of and how they produce fruit.

Each apple blossom begins with a little knob at the end of a stem. Five green *sepals* (SEE-pulz) grow out of the knob, and above them are five pinkish white *petals*. They spread out around the *pistil,* which consists of a ball-shaped base and five slender necks whose technical name is *styles.* Around the pistil are about twenty *stamens* (STAY-menz), whose thread-like stalks end in thick *anthers.* The stalks of the stamens are white, but the anthers are pale yellow or purple.

The process of making apples begins when pollen gets onto a pistil. We sometimes call pollen "dust" or "grains," but pollen grains are living cells that develop inside anthers. When the anthers open, the cells spill out. Most of them go to other

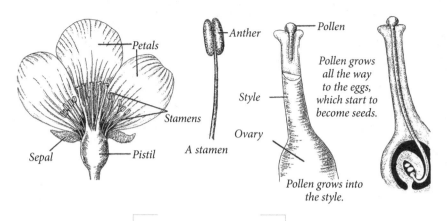

Petals

Anther

Pollen

Stamens

Style

Pollen grows
all the way
to the eggs,
which start to
become seeds.

Ovary

Sepal

Pistil

A stamen

Pollen grows into
the style.

Parts of an apple blossom

flowers or even to other trees.

Some kinds of trees have dry, lightweight pollen that easily floats through the air. Apple pollen is heavier and is rather sticky. It needs help in order to go to another blossom.

Help comes from the bees and flower flies. When these insects crawl into apple blossoms, pollen always sticks to their heads, bodies, and forelegs. When a bee or fly visits another flower, some pollen is sure to stick to the pistil.

The pollen lies there for a while and then begins to grow. Each cell sends out a tiny, root-like tube that grows downward through the soft, pulpy style. Soon the tubes reach several egg cells in the swollen base of the *pistil*, which is the ovary. The eggs then develop into seeds, while the ovary becomes an apple.

We call the apple a fruit and eat it. Oranges, plums, and cherries also have juicy fruit that is good to eat, but many other fruits are dry or hard. Maple "seeds," for example, are dry fruits with wing-like sails. Acorns are hard as well as dry, and so are hickory nuts. Walnuts have pulpy outer coats, but hard shells cover the seeds.

Apple blossoms produce both eggs and pollen. So do the
flowers on dogwoods, tulip trees, black locusts, and some
kinds of maple. Other flowers have only stamens or pistils and
produce only pollen or eggs. The *staminate* flowers are called
males, while the *pistillate* are females. Both types generally
are so small that we do not notice them. Sugar maples, oaks,
and hickories are familiar trees that have tiny staminate or
pistillate flowers.

Have you ever seen a pine flower? It is too small to be called
a blossom, for it has no sepals or petals. The male flowers are
found in small, slender cones. Female cones are shorter and
thicker, and the flowers have no styles. The eggs are hidden
under scales, and the pollen sifts or is blown under them.
The eggs then develop into seeds, while the scales of the cone
become thick and woody. When the scales also harden and turn
brown, we say that the cone is ripe.

*Fruits of several kinds. Five of them grow upon trees.*

Cherry

Raspberry

White oak

Lemon

Fig

Milkweed

Hickory

Pine flowers have no sweet nectar, and their pollen is not good to eat. Because of this, no insects visit them and carry their pollen about.

This does not bother the pine trees, for their pollen floats in the air. Much of it settles to the ground or falls upon other plants. But millions and millions of cells are produced. Some of them are sure to reach the female flowers and start the development of eggs.

Pines have no special means of catching pollen that falls upon the cones. But many female flowers whose pollen is brought by the wind have pistils with sticky or feathery tips. Male flowers often hang in tassels that sway back and forth, shaking their pollen into the air. Oak trees, for example, have male flowers that hang in tassels. Female oak flowers grow in prickly bunches that nestle close to the twigs.

Most flowers whose pollen is carried by wind are also very small. The air can bring living cells to them as well as it can to blossoms as large as poppies or tulips.

Other trees, whose pollen is carried by insects, have flowers with sweet nectar and pollen that is good to eat. These flowers also smell sweet or are brightly colored. Both odors and colors attract hungry insects. The flowers are like signs saying, "Come and eat!" They don't have to say anything about price, for the insects pay when they rub pollen from the stamen of one blossom onto the pistil of another.

# SEEDS AND THEIR TRAVELS

Several clumps of cottonwoods grew upon a Western plain. Except for some Chinese elms near a ranch house, they were the only trees to be seen.

Cottonwoods grow in many places, from Alaska to Mexico and from California to Quebec. These special trees were plains cottonwoods, which live east of the Rocky Mountains and west of the Missouri River. Plains cottonwoods are shorter than their eastern relatives, which often grow more than 80 feet tall. Leaves of the Western variety are thick, pale green and shiny, and are about three inches long. Their tips are pointed, and their edges have coarse, rounded teeth.

Since cottonwoods need plenty of water, they generally grow in low places. In pioneer times, people who traveled across the Western plains always watched for cottonwoods. They knew that the trees marked ponds or creeks where horses and oxen could drink, and where water barrels could be filled.

These particular clumps of plains cottonwoods stood on the banks of a river that came from the foothills near the Rocky Mountains. In summer, the river sometimes ran dry, and the soil on its banks became hard. If several weeks went by without rain, the cottonwood leaves turned yellow and fell to the ground.

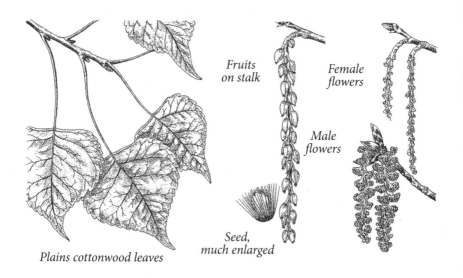

*Fruits on stalk*

*Female flowers*

*Male flowers*

*Seed, much enlarged*

*Plains cottonwood leaves*

The trees remained bare all winter, while snow piled up among the foothills and drifted high on the plains. When snowdrifts melted and spring rains began, the river filled and overflowed. Then the cottonwoods stood in water, and rubbish drifted against their trunks. Soon the trees began to develop flowers, which came before the leaves appeared.

Cottonwood flowers grow upon catkins. So do the flowers of poplars, aspens, and willows, for all these trees belong to the willow family. A catkin has a central stalk and tiny flowers without petals. While the first flowers bloom, the stalk grows longer and more flowers appear. This continues until the catkins of some trees become eight inches long.

The largest cottonwood that stood near the river had thousands of long, slender catkins, and every one bore female flowers. Thicker, shorter catkins, whose flowers were male, grew upon nearby trees. Every breeze that shook the male catkins loosened small clouds of pollen. It soon floated to the female flowers and fertilized their eggs.

When the male catkins lost their pollen, they fell to the ground. The female catkins stayed on their tree while their eggs developed into seeds and the catkins grew longer and longer. At last they looked like slender tassels with seed pods instead of flowers.

The cottonwood seeds ripened in June. Each one was a brown particle with a tuft of cottony threads. Several seeds were packed into every pod. There they stayed until wind swung the catkins, slapping them against twigs and leaves until the pods opened. The wind caught their threads as the seeds came out and quickly whirled them away. Some seeds floated for miles before they came to the ground.

But wasn't this bad for the seeds? Didn't the wind take them to dry places where they could not grow?

The answers to these questions are both yes and no. Many seeds did sail far from the river and were left in places where they soon died. But the wind also dropped some seeds on damp ground, away from other trees. These seeds could sprout and send out roots and could grow upward in bright sunshine. They could not have done this if they had fallen under the full-grown cottonwood trees.

All members of the willow family have tufted seeds that float in the wind. Sycamore seeds are tufted, too, but the tufts are like hairs, not cotton. Sycamore flowers also grow in tufts, and their ball-shaped fruits become ripe in the fall. They hang on the trees for several months, but then fall late in the winter or in spring.

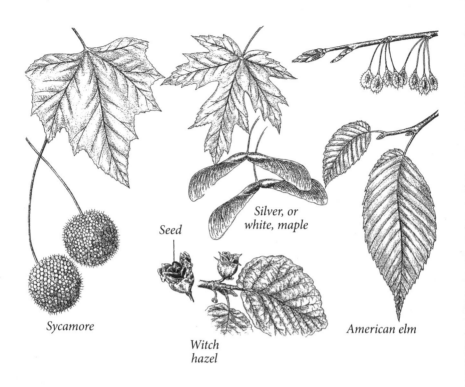

Seed

Silver, or
white, maple

Sycamore

Witch
hazel

American elm

Elm and maple seeds travel by means of wings that are part
of the fruit. An elm fruit's wing is very thin and spreads out
around the seed. When wind blows against this wing, the seed
sails away through the air.

Maple wings also are thin, but they spread out at only one
side. Since two "seeds," or fruits, always cling together, they
have a pair of wings. When the fruits fall, they whirl round and
round and drift sideways with the wind.

Tree fruits or seeds often fall upon water, which carries
them to new homes. If you watch a creek that flows through a
woodland, you may find seeds of elms, maples, or beech trees
floating on the water. Even acorns and walnuts will be carried
downstream if they fall into the creek.

Coconut palms often grow on the shores of tropical islands. Their seeds, which are nuts, are covered with hard shells and fibrous coats that float easily. When coconuts fall into the ocean, tides and currents carry them away. Some of them never do come to land, but others are washed onto distant beaches where they are able to grow. This is one of the reasons why coconut palms are found on islands that are far from other lands.

Birds, people, and other creatures also scatter the seeds of various trees.

Inside of a cherry, there is a hard "stone" which holds the cherry seed. A robin can swallow cherries, but he cannot digest their stones. They pass through the bird's body unharmed and fall to the ground in his droppings. In that way, cherry stones are scattered far from the trees on which they grow. Plums and

*Jack pine*

*Lodgepole pine*

*Sweet gum*

*Sweet gum seeds develop in burs, but pine seeds are found in cones. Seeds of jack pines and lodgepole pines often stay in their cones for years.*

peaches also have hard, stone-like pits. Have you ever eaten a peach and thrown the pit away? That is one way in which cultivated fruit trees "go wild." When raccoons, opossums, or other animals drop the pits of wild fruits, they also have a chance to grow in places where they did not live before.

Acorns are the fruits of oak trees. Squirrels that eat acorns often gather more than they need. They bury or hide the extra acorns for use at some later time, but they do not always find them again. Acorns that have been hidden in the ground all winter are ready to grow when spring comes. Beech trees, walnuts, and hickories also grow from seeds which squirrels hide in the ground and then forget to eat. These trees grow best in sunny places, but oak seedlings do well in the shade.

Witch hazels that grow in thick woods become small bushes, but those that live in open places sometimes grow 20 to 30 feet high. The seeds are covered by hard brown cases that look a good deal like nuts. When autumn comes, the cases shrink and shrink. At last they snap open at one end and shoot the seeds out into the air. In this way, the seeds travel to places in which they find room to grow.

Sweet gum seeds develop in round, spiny burs that hang from string-like stems. Small holes open in the burs after the seeds ripen. When wind blows the burs, they dance on their strings and shake out the seeds.

Pine seeds, as you know, are found in cones made of hard, overlapping scales. The cone scales lie tightly against each other until it is time for the seeds to start growing. Then the scales spread apart, and the ripe seeds drop out. Some kinds of pines have cones that open on the tree. Other cones fall to the ground before they open.

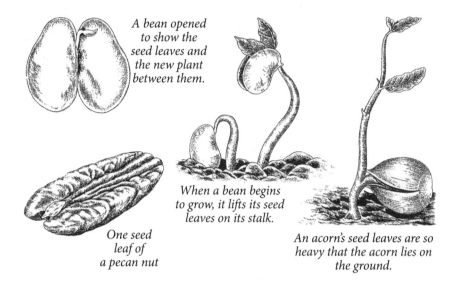

*A bean opened to show the seed leaves and the new plant between them.*

*When a bean begins to grow, it lifts its seed leaves on its stalk.*

*One seed leaf of a pecan nut*

*An acorn's seed leaves are so heavy that the acorn lies on the ground.*

Seed leaves contain food which young plants use when they grow.

Cones of the sand pine, which grows in Florida, stay on the tree for several years. At last the cones open on very hot days, or when fire breaks out in the forest. Fire kills most of the growing trees, but it also makes the cones of sand pines open, letting the seeds fall out. They soon sprout and begin to grow into a new forest. Lodgepole pines and jack pines also have cones that open after fires. Lodgepole pines are found in the West, from South Dakota to the Pacific Coast. Jack pines range from Minnesota to Maine and northward into Canada. Jack pine cones sometimes stay on the trees for more than twenty years.

We sometimes think that seeds are bits or lumps of living material with no special parts or structures. Actually, every fertile seed contains a tiny plant that has developed from an egg. This plant contains the beginnings of a stem and a root. They are covered by either one or two structures that are very special leaves that have become storage places for food. The old plant fills them with starch, sugar, and fat. The new plant that is hidden away in the seed uses this stored-up food when it begins to grow.

These storage structures, called *cotyledons* (KOT-i-LEE -dunz), or seed leaves, may be smooth or deeply wrinkled. They also contain more fat than many other seeds.

Most tree seeds have two seed leaves, but coconuts and other palm seeds have one. So do lily seeds and grass seeds, as well as rice, wheat, oats, and kernels of corn. This explains why we said, on page 7, that palms are related to these small plants, but not to oaks, maples, and pines.

# HOW TREES START TO GROW

A thicket of birch trees stood on a hillside. Their oval leaves had jagged, irregular teeth, and the bark on their trunks was white marked with black. In places where the bark had split, it peeled off like curls of paper.

Seeds of these paper birches were small, with two rounded wings. The seeds developed in cone-like structures about an inch long, and they ripened in the fall. Soon they dropped out of the cones and fluttered or sailed to the ground.

Birds and mice ate hundreds of the birch seeds, but many more remained. They lay among pebbles and under dead leaves or were hidden away in the grass. There they stayed until the warmth of springtime gave them a chance to grow.

One seed that was not eaten lay upon a flat pebble and was covered by a dead leaf. When spring came, the seed began to germinate. This means that it softened and swelled until its brown cover split open. Out came a pointed white root which started to grow toward the ground. But the pebble was in its way, so the root had to turn and grow sideways. Soon it came to the edge of the stone and grew downward again. At last it pushed its way into the soil by twisting like a corkscrew.

While the root twisted into the ground, a white stem began to grow upward. As it grew, it pushed the dead leaf out of the way. The stem also lifted the two seed leaves, which still were partly filled with food. They spread out below the first green leaves that grew on the tiny tree. When those green leaves began to make food, the seed leaves withered away.

Though thousands of birch seeds sprouted, all but a few of the seedlings soon died. Hard rain storms washed some out of the ground and drowned others that grew in low places. Still others were killed by the hot summer sunshine, and many were eaten by rabbits. One rabbit even nibbled the seedling beside the pebble, but a noise frightened the creature away.

After that, the little tree had no trouble. It got all the water it needed, as well as dissolved minerals. An old, tall birch sheltered it at midday when the sun was hottest. Yet light

*Leaves, bark, and a seed of the paper birch. The seed is about three times life size.*

*Gray birch*

*Sweet birch*

*River, or
black, birch*

*Yellow birch*

*Leaves and seeds of four kinds of birch
trees. The seeds are several times life size.*

reached the seedling's green leaves, which made plenty of food.
The seedling grew with part of the food and stored what was left
for use the next spring.

Paper birches are often called "canoe birches" because early
Native Americans used the bark of large trees to cover canoes.
River, or black, birches have reddish-brown bark and are often
grown in parks. Gray birches are either gray or white, and their
leaves end in slender points. Yellow birches have trunks two to
three feet thick and are often cut for lumber. Their wood is very
hard and strong, and makes sturdy furniture.

Gray birches are often the first trees to grow after fire has
destroyed a grove or forest. If the birches are plentiful, they
form thickets where bushes and other young trees soon appear.
Birds nest in the thickets, too, or come there for shelter and
food in the winter. The birds eat berries that stay on the bushes
or pick up birch seeds from the ground.

Young maples and oaks, and many young conifers, need protection from bright sunshine and wind. They cannot grow in open places, but they do very well in birch thickets. When the birches finally begin to die, these other trees are growing well. They also make such thick shade that young birches cannot get a start. In this way, the birch thicket disappears while a forest of oaks grows up in its place.

Most trees begin to grow on the ground, where their roots can burrow into moist soil. But mangroves start out above the earth's surface, and so do many trees and bushes in forests of the Northwest.

Red mangroves are small trees that live along warm, marshy sea coasts. Seeds germinate while the fruits are still on the trees, sending out plump roots that grow to be a foot or more in length. When these seedlings fall, they drop into the water. There they float with their roots below the surface, while their stems point upward.

*Red mangrove trees on a swampy seacoast. Roots are growing from two fruits that hang on a twig.*

Mangrove seedlings may float for days till the roots anchor themselves to the bottom. After that, the trees grow rapidly—and then comes another change. Roots grow downward from each mangrove tree's branches, while the lower part of its stem dies and decays. Soon the tree stands only upon these roots, which look like curved stilts. They keep the leaves safely above high tides, which would soon kill them.

Trees in rainy forests near the northern Pacific Coast stand on stilts that form in a different way. There, seeds often germinate on top of stumps or in the moss that covers huge logs. Roots grow into the decaying woods, where they get all the water they need. But in time, the roots reach into the ground, while the stumps and logs crumble away. This leaves the trees on stilt-like roots that may stand as much as 8 or 10 feet above the surrounding soil.

*The seedling at the left is growing on top of a stump left by lumbermen. At the right is a good-sized tree, but the trunk on which it once stood has decayed, leaving the roots above the ground. The tree below has grown from a "stool" that has been partly covered by new wood and bark.*

Young trees that grow from seeds are called seedlings until they become two or three feet tall. Then we generally call them saplings. But new trees do not always grow from seeds. They may also come from roots and twigs or from stumps, and some even grow from leaves.

Willow trees will grow from twigs that are stuck into wet soil. If pussy-willow branches are kept in water, they will sprout small white roots. Then the branches can be planted in the ground.

When a tree is chopped down, twigs and leaves often sprout from the stump. Sometimes one twig grows straight upward, becoming a new trunk. Several twigs also may become large, spreading out above the stump, or "stool," which is often covered by new bark and new wood.

If a tree is chopped off very close to the ground, it may sprout again from the roots. Such sprouts grow faster than seedlings do, for they have many large roots to provide them with water and minerals.

Redwoods that live near the Pacific Coast are famous for their ability to send up new trunks from roots. If you look in a redwood grove, you will see rings of trunks that grew from the roots of old trees and kept growing after they died. You can also see new trees that have grown from the roots of stumps that were cut 60 or even 90 years ago. Some of these new trees are almost large enough to be cut down and sawed into lumber.

# TREES IN THE WINTER

Snow fell on a horse chestnut tree that stood in a park. Some white flakes touched the branches and then fell off. Other flakes stayed in the crotches where twigs grew from branches or where one large branch divided into two.

Horse chestnuts are not chestnuts, in spite of their name. They are relatives of small trees called buckeyes, which grow wild in various parts of the United States. But horse chestnuts once lived in Asia and southeastern Europe. Seeds were taken to France and England and then to North America.

Many people like horse chestnuts because they have clusters of showy white flowers that are spotted with yellow and purple. Horse chestnut leaves are showy, too, for they are large and dark green. They are also compound, with five to seven leaflets that spread out at the end of a stem. Some leaflets become eight inches long, and the whole leaves are 12 to 15 inches wide.

When autumn came, the horse chestnut's leaves turned yellowish brown and then fell to the ground. Soon the tree looked like a skeleton made of a trunk that divided into thick branches about six feet above the ground. These main branches grew upward, but others spread out sideways. Only their tips turned and began to grow upward again.

Large reddish-brown flower buds grew at the ends of the twigs. Smaller leaf buds grew opposite one another along the sides of the twigs. The side buds on maple twigs also grow in opposite pairs, but many trees have alternate buds. Such buds grow one on one side of the twig and then one on the other. A willow twig shows this arrangement plainly.

Snow stopped falling upon the horse chestnut, and the wind began to blow. It shook snow caps from the big flower buds and swept snow from the branches.

As the wind continued to blow, the air became colder and colder. It froze the surface of the snowdrifts on the ground into a hard crust. Moisture on the bark of the tree also froze, becoming little slivers of ice. One twig had been broken and torn back by the wind. There the cold air froze both the inner bark and the delicate cambium cells.

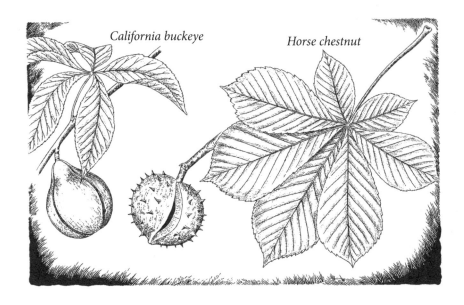

*California buckeye*          *Horse chestnut*

Cold did not harm the leaves and beginnings of flowers that were hidden in the horse chestnut buds. Each bud had a shiny cover that protected it, just as layers of bark protected the branches and twigs. The bud cover was also coated with a sticky varnish that kept moisture out.

Roots of the horse chestnut were protected by soil and snow. Many roots went deep into the ground, where the soil never became very cold. Other roots spread out near the surface. Snow that covered the ground kept roots near the surface from freezing, for cold air could not get to the ground.

Warm sunshine began to melt the snow a few days after the storm. In one place, some frozen pansy plants appeared. There also were bushes and young holly trees whose branches had broken under the snow that had clung to them. But the horse chestnut was safe. When spring came, its buds would unfold and become leaves or flowers. Its roots also would grow and soak up moisture, and most of the twigs would become longer. The broken twig with torn bark was the only one that died.

Shall we open a horse chestnut bud to find out how it is formed? First, we peel off the reddish-brown scales of the outer bud cover, with its coat of waterproof varnish. Then comes the inner bud cover, made of green scales that resemble leaves.

When the green scales have been peeled off too, the bud looks white and furry. The "fur" is a cottony pad which protects the buds from bumps and from becoming too cold.

We now pull the cottony pad aside. Under it are four tiny leaves with five to seven leaflets. Each one is folded down the middle and is wrapped up with its neighbors. There is padding in every fold and between the leaflets.

All trees have winter buds that contain young leaves and flowers. Some kinds, such as apple trees, may put both leaves and blossoms together in a single bud. Other trees keep them separate, as they are on the horse chestnut.

The flowering dogwood is a tree whose flowers and leaves are in separate buds. Leaf buds are flat, but flower buds are ball-shaped, and they turn white or pink in the spring. The scales of these flower buds do not fall off when they open, but spread out and grow. Soon they become what people often (but wrongly) call the petals of dogwood blossoms. The real flowers are small, yellow things that grow near the center of the four white or pink scales.

The winter buds of different trees have different shapes, and they open in various ways. The dogwood leaf bud has two scales instead of four, and they spread apart like the beak of a bird. Willow buds have only one scale, which breaks off and

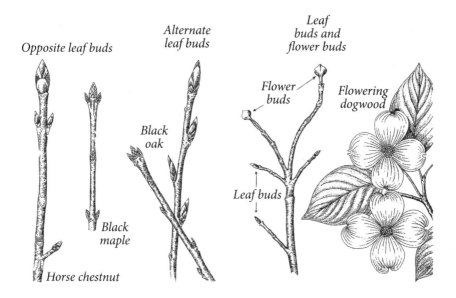

Opposite leaf buds

Alternate leaf buds

Leaf buds and flower buds

Flower buds

Flowering dogwood

Black oak

Black maple

Leaf buds

Horse chestnut

falls to the ground. Scales of peach buds are arranged in spirals. The buds seem to unwind as the scales open one by one.

Just below the buds on horse chestnut wings are scars made when dead leaves broke away. Each leaf scar is shaped somewhat like a horseshoe, and dots near the edge of the scar look like nail marks. The dots actually show where the tubes that carried sap extended into the leaf while it was on the tree.

Leaf scars on other trees are shaped differently. Maple scars are curved like quarter-moons. Scars on butternut and hickory twigs look like hearts.

Dark streaks or dashes on the branches of young horse chestnuts are the lenticels. Trees can breathe with their leaves in the summer, but when winter comes and leaves fall off, lenticels must be used. Though such breathing is so slight that you cannot hear it or feel it, it helps to keep the tree alive.

While trees breathe through lenticels, they also lose some water. In the summer that loss is not important. But when winter's cold freezes moisture in the soil, roots cannot get water to replace what is lost. Because of this, trees may dry out and die before spring comes again.

Evergreen trees, such as pines and holly, lose water from their leaves as well as their lenticels. If an evergreen gets too much sunlight or grows in a cold, windy place, its leaves may dry out and turn brown. Even if the tree is not killed, the brown leaves are dead.

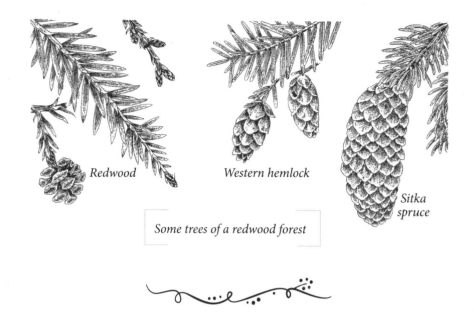

*Redwood*  *Western hemlock*  *Sitka spruce*

Some trees of a redwood forest

# WHERE TREES LIVE

Fog was coming in along the coast of northern California. The low, misty clouds covered the beaches and towns and spread over forests of redwoods, hemlocks, and spruces. Soon the treetops were almost hidden in dull, grayish haze.

Most trees in the forest were tall, but the redwoods were tallest. Many were 200 to 250 feet high, and one was more than 300. Its trunk spread out near the ground and then grew straight upward. It was 15 to 20 feet thick and was covered with bark that had split into deep furrows and coarse ridges. The bark was reddish brown inside, but its surface was gray.

You might expect such a tree to have large leaves and seeds. But the redwood's leaves were flat needles, one-fourth to three-fourths of an inch in length. The seeds, with their wings, were not much larger than this letter O, and the cones were less than one inch long. They were about half as long as the cones of jack pines, which may be only 15 feet high.

Water droplets began to settle on needles as the fog spread over the redwoods. Soon the droplets ran together and formed drops which dripped onto the ground. It almost seemed as if rain were sprinkling down through the trees.

The drops of water were not rain, nor were the droplets of fog. But both were very, very important. Redwoods live where heavy rains fall in winter, but the long summers are dry. There is water in the ground, of course, and the redwood roots can get it. But they could not get nearly enough if the ground dried out rapidly. They also could not get enough if the needle-shaped leaves were losing water in dry, hot, sunny air.

This is where foggy weather helps. The fog itself moistens the air, shuts out sunshine, and keeps the forest cool. That cuts down evaporation from the needles and so keeps them from losing water faster than the roots can get it. Drops that fall from the needles moisten the ground, which stays damp and cool under the shady forest. Moist, cool soil loses so little water that plenty is left for the trees.

You can see how important fog is to redwoods if you drive along the coast southward from San Francisco. There the fog often goes up deep valleys or canyons, but it does not cover the mountains between them. Redwoods grow in the damp, foggy canyons, but the mountains are covered with grass and wild oats, with scattered groves of buckeyes, oaks, and Douglas fir. They live well in dry places where no redwood can grow.

The kind of place in which a plant or animal lives is called its *habitat*. The redwood's habitat is a belt of foggy valleys and hills near the Pacific Ocean. Another species of redwood, the "Big Tree," or giant sequoia, is found among mountain valleys

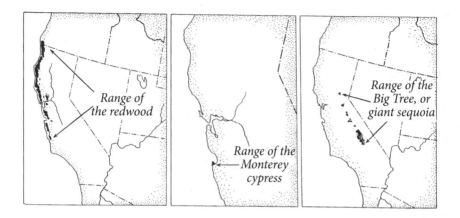

*Range of the redwood*

*Range of the Monterey cypress*

*Range of the Big Tree, or giant sequoia*

where there is little fog and the air becomes very dry. Deep snows fill the ground with moisture that lasts through the summer months.

The bald cypress grows best in wet ground where the air is both moist and warm. The tree finds these conditions in Southern swamps, which are its habitat. Another conifer, the black spruce, needs cool weather and damp ground. It lives in swampy places from Minnesota and New Jersey to Alaska. Whitebark pines live on mountains of the West, where the soil is thin, the weather grows cold, and the wind blows almost every day. Only a few other trees share the whitebark pine's habitat.

Several kinds of trees grow best in dry places or even deserts. One of these is the palo verde, whose green bark makes food when the tree has no leaves. The smoketree also has a desert habitat, though it generally grows in "washes" where streams flow for a while after it rains. The smoketree's bark has a hairy coat that keeps water from evaporating.

The whole region in which one kind of plant or animal lives is its range. The ranges of some trees are surprisingly small. Redwoods, for example, are found near the coast of northern

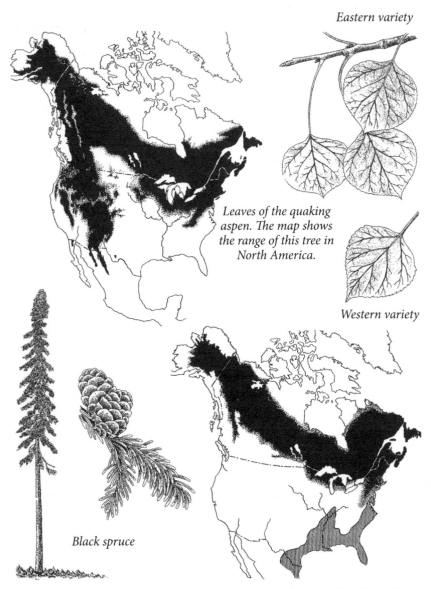

*Eastern variety*

Leaves of the quaking
aspen. The map shows
the range of this tree in
North America.

*Western variety*

*Black spruce*

Ranges of the black spruce (black) and bald
cypress (lines)

California and a short way into Oregon. Sequoias live on some western slopes of the Sierra Nevada, and the Monterey cypress grows wild near the city of Monterey, California. Trees in other regions were planted there and are outside their natural range.

The quaking aspen is a species whose range is very large. Aspens are found from northwestern Alaska to Mexico, and from California to Newfoundland. A closely related species inhabits northern Europe and Asia.

Aspens have wide ranges because they can live in different habitats and under different conditions. They grow in moist ground near ponds and on plains too dry for cottonwoods. Aspens are common on some sea coasts and on many mountains, some of which are surrounded by deserts. The trees also thrive where summers become very hot, as well as where winters are cold. There are fine aspen groves in places where the temperature drops more than 60 degrees below zero.

White oaks can also stand very cold or very hot weather. Although they grow best on moist ground near streams, they are found on higher, dried land and on stony ridges. We are not surprised to discover that white oaks range from eastern Canada to Florida and from Oklahoma to Maine. Still, there are some habitats in which these trees cannot live. You will never find white oaks on sandy seashores, for example, or on steep, stony mountainsides.

The weather on very high mountains becomes too cold and windy for trees of any kind. The place where they stop growing is called the *timberline*. In general, the timberline is very high on southern mountains, but it becomes lower and lower in the north.

At last the climate becomes so cold that trees cannot grow on mountains at all or even upon low ground. The place where this happens is generally called the *tree line*. The black spruce is one of the trees that ranges northward to the tree line and then stops. The tamarack is another. In many places, these trees stand up straight and are 30 to 50 feet tall. But at the tree line, they are little and twisted. A spruce that has grown for a 100 years near the tree line may be less than three feet in height.

*Three trees that grow on mountains, up to timberline:*

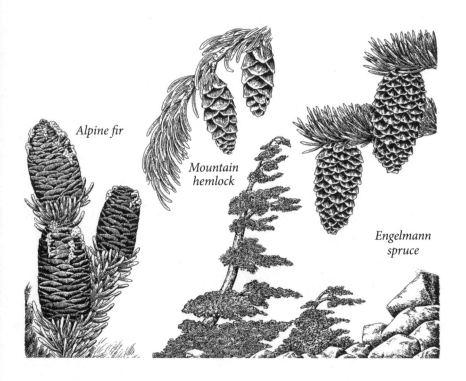

Alpine fir

Mountain
hemlock

Engelmann
spruce

# TREES DIFFER

Wind blew across a western mountain. On bare slopes it became a howling gale, but big rocks and steep ridges slowed it down. In the shelter of one ridge, the wind sank into a breeze that made sighing sounds in a limber pine.

Since spring had come, new shoots were growing at the tips of the pine branches. The shoots were pale green and looked so waxy that people sometimes called them "candles." A ring, or whorl, of new twigs grew outward around each candle.

No wind could blow the limber pine over, for its strong taproot went deep into the ground. In its sheltered home, the pine stood up straight, and branches spread out all around its trunk. The tree also was able to grow quite rapidly. Sometimes it became 12 inches taller during a single year.

Other limber pines lived on slopes where nothing sheltered them from the wind. It pushed the trunks until they leaned sideways and grew at a slant. Wind bent the growing branches, too, but it seldom broke them. They were so tough that they could bend again and again, which explains why this particular species of tree is called the *limber* pine.

Although the growing branches were limber, the candles at their tips were not. Gales snapped the ends from many candles and broke others below their rings of new twigs. This kept the trees from becoming tall but allowed some branches to grow sideways. Many of these wind-blown pines developed thick, short trunks that leaned away from the wind and had branches that grew in the same direction. Such trees looked as if they were being blown, even when there was no wind.

A few limber pines lived on still higher slopes, up to the timberline. There gales howled almost every day, in summer as well as in winter. They bent young trees until their trunks touched the ground. Winds also snapped off growing candles

*Cone of a limber pine*

*Cone of a whitebark pine*

*The tall limber pine at the right grew in a sheltered place where its branches spread out in all directions. The tree at the left has branches growing away from the wind.*

This limber pine lives where winds are so strong that the branches lie close to the ground.

Winds have bent this tree until it leans to one side. Its branches also grow away from the gales.

The limber pine at the right grew upward until the wind broke off its new shoots. This explains why the tree is not very tall and is almost flat on top.

and whipped twigs to and fro till they died. All this made the pine trees "creep," which means that they spread out on the ground instead of growing upward. Some trees that were 20 to 30 feet long stood less than 4 feet high.

Limber pines range from northern Mexico to Canada, and from South Dakota to California. A few grow on windswept plains, but their favorite habitat is mountains. Whitebark pines are the only other trees that live on such windy slopes.

We have found that limber pines have various shapes, depending upon the winds. Their bark also changes as they grow old. On young trees, it is thin and smooth, and its color is silvery gray. During the middle age, the bark turns gray-brown and cracks into small, irregular sections. The bark of old trunks turns almost black and becomes as much as two inches thick. Its cracks also are longer than those of middle-aged trees.

Limber pines differ, or vary, but we can tell them by their changing bark and by their cones and needles. The needles are less than three inches long, and they always grow in clusters of five. The cones range from 3 to 10 inches in length, and the tips of their scales are blunt. Young cones are reddish purple, but they turn yellowish brown as they ripen.

Whitebark pines are shaped like limber pines, for they grow in similar places. Whitebark needles also grow in clusters of five and are about three inches long. But the bark of these trees does not turn dark, and the cones are no longer than the needles. The cones turn purplish brown when they ripen.

Trees of other kinds also grow where wind breaks their twigs or new shoots. Some of these "wind-sheared" trees have branches on only one side of the trunk. Many other trees lean sideways, and their branches grow uphill. Trees sheltered by huge rocks grow just as high and wide as the stones. Twigs that begin to grow higher are killed by the wind.

Trees that stand alone or in scattered groves can send branches out in all directions, for every branch will get sunlight. But trees in thick forests must grow upward in order to reach sunshine. Such trees become tall and straight, and their lower branches may die. You can easily tell a tall forest oak or maple from the spreading trees of pastures or parks.

Cold weather and poor soil stunt trees, or make them grow very slowly. Aspens that live near the tree line in the north have thin, crooked trunks that are only four to six feet high. Black spruces grow 60 feet high in New Jersey, but those in northern Labrador are only two to four feet tall. Trees that grow on sandy

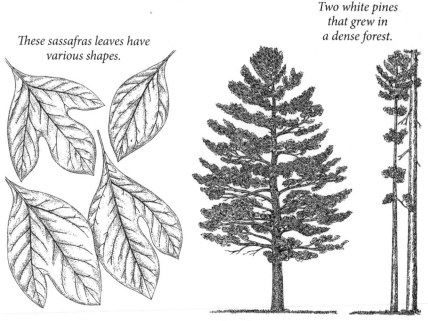

*Two white pines that grew in a dense forest.*

*These sassafras leaves have various shapes.*

*This white pine grew in a meadow.*

shores or dry, rocky places generally are smaller and less healthy than others that live on moist, rich soil.

Other variations come from something in the trees themselves, not from wind, poor soil, or cold weather. Most flowering dogwoods, for example, have white blossoms, but those of some trees are pink. A few honey locusts are almost thornless, and many eastern red cedars become slim, pointed trees with shorter branches than those of the "normal" relatives.

Leaves vary in shape, as well as in size and color. Some white oak leaves are broad, but others are divided into deep, narrow lobes. Sassafras leaves may be oval, but others are divided into two or three lobes that differ in size and shape. A tree may have leaves of only one type, or it may have two or three types on a single branch.

People often grow, or propagate, trees that show attractive variations. Thornless locusts were developed this way. So were "copper" beech trees and several small conifers that are often planted near houses.

We call these new trees "varieties" and give them special names. Other varieties develop naturally, however, without propagation by man. Eastern aspens, for example, have become different from aspens in the West. Plains cottonwoods have smaller leaves than their eastern relatives, and ponderosa pines of the eastern Rocky Mountains have shorter needles than others that grow much farther west. We sometimes call such varieties *subspecies* because they divide the natural kinds, or species, into smaller groups.

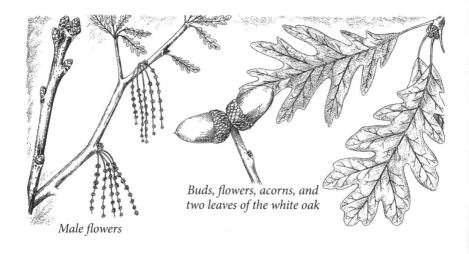

*Buds, flowers, acorns, and two leaves of the white oak*

*Male flowers*

# TREES IN FORESTS

An acorn fell from a tall white oak tree in an eastern forest. The acorn bumped from branch to branch and then dropped to the ground. There it fell so hard that its oblong seed popped out of the rough, shallow cap.

The acorn lay on the ground all winter and sprouted in the spring. First, the shiny seed shell split, and then a white root grew out of the crack. The root turned downward and grew into the soil, which was a mixture of ordinary dirt with decayed wood and leaves. Later, a stem grew upward. It did not take the seed leaves with it, as bean seedlings do. The oak's seed leaves were so heavy that the young stem could not lift them. They had to lie on the ground, inside the broken shell.

Leaves on the forest trees were unfolding when the acorn sprouted. At first they made a light shade on the ground, broken by spots and dashes of sunlight. But while the seedling grew, the leaves became larger, making thicker shade.

The seeds of trees such as cottonwoods, aspens, and lodgepole pines have to sprout where there is sunlight, for they cannot grow in shade. But Western hemlocks need shade while they are seedlings, and so do balsam firs and black spruces. We call cottonwoods *intolerant* but say that black spruces and hemlocks are *tolerant* of shade.

White oaks and many other trees come between these two extremes. They need plenty of sunshine when they grow up, but they sprout and become seedlings in shade. White oak seedlings would die in very strong sunshine, and so would young hickories, beeches, or sugar maples.

Many other acorns also sprouted under the tall white oak tree. When two seedlings lived near one another, their roots grew into the same patch of soil. We say the seedlings *competed* for water, for mineral foods dissolved in it, and for space in which to grow.

You know what happens when two baseball teams compete or struggle against one another. One team gets more bases and home runs than the other and so wins the game.

When the tree seedlings competed, one of them always obtained more water than the other and more minerals. Its leaves produced more sweet food, too, and it grew more rapidly. Soon this seedling won the game of living, and the weaker one died.

This happened again and again under the oak tree and in other parts of the forest. Thousands of seedlings died, but other thousands lived and grew into saplings. They also began to need more sunlight, but the old trees still shaded them. The

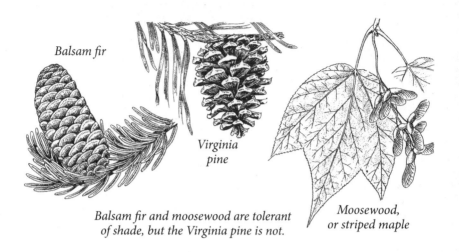

*Balsam fir*

*Virginia pine*

*Balsam fir and moosewood are tolerant of shade, but the Virginia pine is not.*

*Moosewood, or striped maple*

saplings could not grow rapidly except in the spring, before the full-grown trees had "leafed out."

Several years went by while the old trees shaded the saplings, which grew very slowly. But at last a great windstorm swept through the forest. It did not harm the saplings, which were near the ground where it could not reach them. But the tall trees swayed in the wind, which snapped off twigs, broke branches, and blew away great numbers of leaves.

Oaks have such long taproots that healthy trees are seldom blown down. But the tall white oak was very old, and it was not healthy. Shelf fungi had eaten most of its heartwood, and root fungi had weakened its roots. As the wind kept on blowing, the taproot broke and let the oak tip sideways. Soon its hollow trunk split, and its branches crashed to the ground.

Light flooded into the forest after the old oak fell. Sunshine brightened the leaves of the saplings, which were larger than the leaves of full-grown trees and could make more food. Soon the saplings were growing rapidly—and once more they began to compete. Those that won grew tall, sent out strong branches, and in time became large trees. They shaded the weaker, less fortunate saplings, which either were stunted or died.

A few dozen trees may make up a grove, but thousands or millions of trees live together in a forest. If most of them belong to one species, we say that they form a *pure stand*. You may have seen pure stands of ponderosa or lodgepole pines in the West, or of cypresses in Southern forests. But most forests contain several kinds of trees that live together, just as people

*There are three "layers" of plants in a pine forest. Pine trees form the highest layer, while small shrubs and grasses make up the lowest. The middle layer consists of partly grown trees.*

of different names and races live near each other in cities.
Engelmann spruces, for example, often grow among lodgepole
pines. Oaks, hemlocks, beeches, and maples may be found side
by side in the forests of the East.

When we walk through a forest, we find that its trees and
smaller plants are divided into three layers. The first layer
consists of full-grown trees, which stand so high that their tops
get sunshine on every bright day. They also shade plants that
grow nearer to the ground.

The second layer contains young trees that are too large to
be called saplings but still are not very tall. These young trees,
and other kinds that are older, are tolerant of shade. Engelmann
spruces need the shade they get from pines, and balsam firs
grow very well in the shelter of tall beeches and maples. The
broad-leafed maple, a Western species, can even live in the
dense shade under redwoods, though it grows best in sunnier

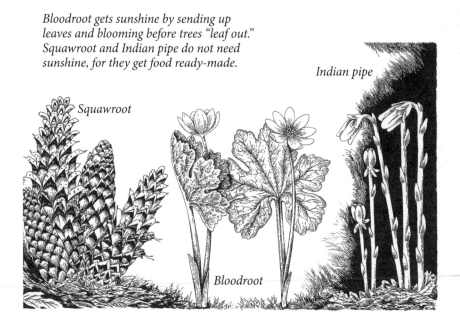

*Bloodroot gets sunshine by sending up
leaves and blooming before trees "leaf out."
Squawroot and Indian pipe do not need
sunshine, for they get food ready-made.*

*Indian pipe*

*Squawroot*

*Bloodroot*

places. But many ferns grow only in shady places, while others wilt and become stunted if the trees above them die.

The third forest layer is made up of plants and other things that live on the ground or only grow a few inches above it. The oxalis in redwood forests belongs here. So do mushrooms, trilliums, Mayapples, and a host of other small plants. Slugs are members of the third layer, too, along with chipmunks, salamanders, and ground-dwelling insects.

Rhododendrons and laurels show how tolerant plants also make use of sunshine. They are shrubs of the forests' second layer, and their thick leaves can make food in shade. Still, the plants need sunshine when they bloom. They get it by blooming early in the spring, before the leaves of oaks, maples, and other trees have become very large.

Small plants that belong to the third layer may bloom even earlier. Bloodroots, hepaticas, and spring beauties open their flowers in March or April. At that time, bright spring sunshine comes down through the branches. It warms the plants that live there, as well as the insects that carry their pollen.

The Indian pipe and squawroot have found ways of living without sunshine. The Indian pipe is waxy white and cannot make sugary food. Most species soak up food as well as water from decayed wood and leaves that cover the ground. But the pale-brown squawroot has become a parasite. Its roots grow into those of trees and absorb their sap.

*American elm*

*An elm bark beetle seen through a magnifying glass*

# WHY TREES DIE

A bark beetle alighted upon an elm tree. The insect walked along a branch to a crotch where the branch divided. There the beetle lowered its head and began to bite into the soft juicy bark.

While the insect was feeding, another bark beetle came and sat down beside it. Both were smaller than ground beetles or June "bugs," for they were only one-eighth of an inch long. The hard coats on their bodies were reddish brown, and so were the two "shells" that covered their delicate wings.

As the beetles ate, their jaws cut a narrow, irregular hole through the bark and into the elm tree's sapwood. The beetles pushed to and fro in the hole until specks of dust came off their bodies and stuck to the wood.

Those specks were not ordinary dust but were spores that had come from a fungus. A fungus is a living thing that grows like a plant, and its spores do the work of seeds. They come from an old fungus and are carried to places where they can grow into new ones. Some of them float through the air, but many are carried about by insects or other small animals.

The hole which the beetles had cut in the elm tree was just what these spores needed. Soon the spores began to grow, forming thread-like things called *hyphae* (HY-fee), which went deeper and deeper into the sapwood.

Green plants make most of their own food. But a fungus is not green, which means it has no food-making chlorophyll. Because of this, the fungus has to get its food from other plants or animals. If a fungus feeds upon dead things, it may be useful, for it destroys rubbish. But if a fungus gets food from something that is living, it becomes a parasite. Parasites often damage their victims so badly that they die.

Spores that came from the bark beetles belonged to the parasitic fungus that causes Dutch elm disease. As this fungus grew, its thread-like hyphae clogged the sapwood of two twigs. This meant that the wood could not take watery sap to the leaves. The leaves soon turned yellow and fell, and then the twigs themselves died. Before the summer ended, several branches, as well as twigs, had been killed by the fungus.

A female bark beetle came to the tree soon after the first branch died. She gnawed a tunnel under the bark and laid eggs along the sides. Then she crept out of the tunnel and flew away. Soon the eggs hatched into tiny white grubs that burrowed through the branch and ate its dead inner bark.

The grubs rested in their burrows during the winter. In the spring, they woke up and began to eat and grow. When they could grow no more, they became hard-shelled *pupae*. Inside those shells, the pupae turned into beetles, which crawled out of their pupa shells and chewed tunnels to the surface of the branch. They sat for a while and then flew away, leaving fungus spores on other elm trees when they stopped to eat.

While fungus parasites began to grow in new elms, the disease kept on spreading through the first tree. Leaves turned yellow and fell from branch after branch as fungus threads killed their sapwood. When the leaves on the last branch withered, the sick tree finally died.

The elm bark beetle kills trees by leaving spores of fungi in them. Other beetles gnaw tunnels as they feed upon cambium, sapwood, and inner bark. This destroys the cambium, loosens the outer bark, and kills trees from the top downward. They die much more quickly than trees that are killed by fungi.

If you look at a tree that has been killed by these beetles, you will see hundreds of burrows in what was once the moist sapwood. A straight tunnel at the center of each burrow was made by the mother beetle when she laid her eggs. Small tunnels that branch from the straight one were made by the

*Burrows of the fruit tree bark beetle (below) and the hickory bark beetle (at right). Both insects are sometimes called engraver beetles.*

grubs as they fed. The grubs then changed into full-grown beetles and crawled out of the tree.

We cannot see the beetles' burrows until a tree dies and the bark begins to fall from its trunk. We do not see the elm disease fungus at all, for it gets its food and grows in the sapwood, where it is completely covered. But some other parasitic funguses (or fungi) show plainly, for they have two different parts. One part consists of the thread-like hyphae, which grow into trees and get food. The other part is pulpy or woody. It grows at the surface of the tree, where it produces spores. They are carried from place to place by the wind, not by insects or other creatures.

Shelf, or bracket, fungi are good examples of these parasites. Some are small and velvety, with pretty markings. Other species are thick and large, and are almost as hard as wood. When we see these spore-bearing "shelves" on a tree trunk, we know that their threads have grown deep into the wood and have made it decay.

Rust fungi get their name because they make orange or reddish brown spots that look like the rust on iron. Rust fungi live on small plants and shrubs, as well as on aspens, apples, cherries, and conifers. One species of rust often kills pine trees by sending hyphae through twigs, branches, and trunks.

Both wild animals and accidents also injure trees or kill them. During the winter, rabbits, porcupines, and field mice often feed on both inner bark and cambium. This leaves bare places where spores of fungi and other disease-makers can get into the wood. The animals may also *girdle* trees, or eat the bark all the way around their trunks. That keeps food sap from going down to the roots, which soon starve to death.

Did you ever examine a tree that has been struck by

lightning? Lightning tears gashes in the bark, makes deep cracks in wood, and even splits trunks in half. Many forest fires also are started by lightning. They kill trees by burning the bark and sapwood or by making them so hot that they die.

Trees have several ways of mending injuries. New leaves grow when old ones are killed by disease or are eaten by insects. Among conifers, pitch oozes out over places where bark has been torn or destroyed. The pitch soon hardens into varnish that keeps fungi from getting into the wood. In both conifers and hardwood trees, cambium builds new bark over damaged places. If you look at trees whose branches have been cut off, or

*Two branches have been cut from this tree. It has covered one stub with new bark and is covering the other.*

*This manzanita tree is dying of old age. Only a little living bark is left on the trunk and on one main branch.*

*Two shelf, or bracket, fungi*

pruned, you will see how bark grows out over the bare wood.

You will also see how human beings help trees to repair injuries. Rough cuts or torn bark heal slowly, and so do stubs of branches. Men who know how to care for trees cut branches close to the trunk and make sure that the bark is not torn. Such men also cover the bare, cut wood with thick paint. It keeps fungus spores from growing before bark can grow over the wound.

Many trees and shrubs that seem to be killed by accidents or diseases really die of old age. The leaves of old trees get less water than leaves of young ones, and they make less food. This means that cambium builds less wood and inner bark and cannot mend injuries so well. Twigs wither and roots become weak; fungi fill sapwood with their threads and make the sturdy heartwood decay. At last, the tree dies or is blown down by winds that could not have harmed it when it was young.

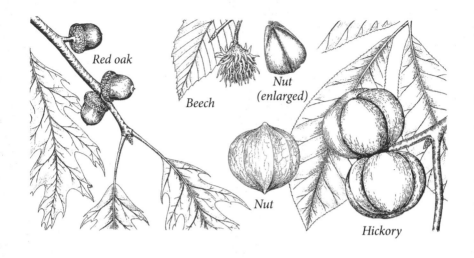

Red oak

Beech

Nut
(enlarged)

Nut

Hickory

# FOOD FROM TREES

A gray squirrel climbed a hickory tree and ran along one of its branches. There he stopped for a moment and chattered. "Chacka-chack!" he said in a voice that sounded as if he were barking at someone he did not like.

Autumn had come, and the hickory tree had lost many of its leaves. Those that still hung from the twigs were bright golden-brown. The leaves also were compound, with five or seven long leaflets arranged on a central stem. The edges of each leaflet were saw-toothed, and the stem had many short hairs.

After chattering, the squirrel looked for a hickory fruit. It was a green ball about two inches long, and its outer part, or husk, had become so hard that it seemed woody.

The squirrel nipped off the fruit with his sharp front teeth and held it between his paws. Next, he broke off the husk, uncovering the pale brown nut. He had to gnaw through the nut's thick shell before he could eat the kernel inside. The kernel was made of two rough parts. Each of them was a seed leaf filled with rich, tasty food.

The squirrel dropped the gnawed pieces of shell, but he ate every bit of the kernel. Then he nipped off another fruit and removed its outer husk. Instead of eating the nut, he held it in his mouth and scampered to the ground. He went so fast that his feet broke small pieces from the shaggy bark.

When the squirrel reached the ground, he ran to a root that grew just above the surface. This left a cup-shaped hollow in which the squirrel stored food for winter. He tucked his nut into the hollow and ran back to the hickory tree.

Hickory nuts are an important food of squirrels in the eastern half of our country. The animals hide nuts away every fall and then dig them up in the winter. Now and then a nut is missed, especially if it is well-hidden away under grass or dead leaves. When spring comes, such nuts begin to grow into new hickory trees.

Other nuts are also eaten by squirrels. The commonest probably are acorns, which may be found in both the East and the West, from Mexico to Canada. Eastern squirrels hide food on the ground, but gray squirrels of the West often store acorns in holes which woodpeckers have pecked into bark. The woodpeckers once stored acorns in the very same holes!

White-footed mice and white-tailed deer are very fond of beech nuts. The nuts are small, with three sides, and they grow in hairy burs. When the burs open, the nuts pop out and fall to the ground, where the deer and the mice find them.

Both wild animals and human beings eat seeds, or nuts, from the cones of the *piñon* (PEEN-yone) and digger pines. Piñon cones and seeds are small, but digger-pine cones grow as much as nine inches long, and their seeds are as large as Spanish peanuts. Indians used to gather them, just as they now gather piñon nuts.

Soft fruits that come from trees are eaten by birds, beasts, and human beings. Everyone knows that robins like cherries, but chipmunks also eat them when they fall to the ground. We use cherries, plums, apples, pears, peaches, and apricots. All these belong to the rose family, but fig trees are related to mulberries, and dates are the fruit of a palm.

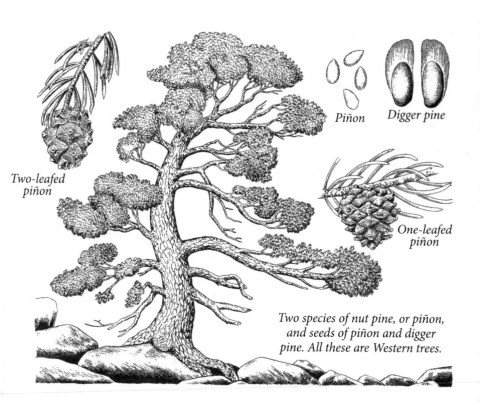

*Piñon*     *Digger pine*

*Two-leafed piñon*

*One-leafed piñon*

*Two species of nut pine, or piñon, and seeds of piñon and digger pine. All these are Western trees.*

*Porcupines eat the inner bark and cambium of trees.*

Many animals eat leaves, twigs, and bark instead of fruit.
During summer, the moose often feeds upon tree leaves, though
he also pulls water plants from ponds. In winter, when broad
leaves have fallen, the big animal feeds on twigs, buds, and even
bark. Elk and deer also eat twigs in the winter when other foods
are scarce.

Leaves are the principal food of young insects called
caterpillars. Though many caterpillars feed on small plants,
some like leaves of oaks, maples, and other broad-leafed trees.
Tent caterpillars, for example, sometimes eat every leaf on wild
cherry trees. When the caterpillars turn into moths and stop
eating, the trees have to grow new leaves.

Bark beetles feed on soft inner bark, while many bugs and
beetles devour tree blossoms and buds. But termites eat dead
wood, and aphids stick their pointed "tongues" into young twigs
and suck sap. If you look closely, you will find insects gnawing,
nibbling, or sucking on almost every tree.

During the summer, porcupines eat tender twigs, as well as leaves and roots of various plants. In winter, the animals may nibble twigs, but they generally gnaw bark and eat its inner layer. Their favorite food is hemlock, but porcupines also eat the inner bark of pines, aspens, and cottonwoods.

Porcupines climb trees and sit in them while they are eating. But beavers cannot climb, so they cut trees down with their strong front teeth. When the tree falls, its trunk and branches are gnawed into sections two to six feet long.

Beavers gnaw the bark from some logs right where they are cut. Others are dragged to streams or ponds and are hidden underwater. When winter comes, the animals take sticks or logs from those hidden piles and feed upon their bark.

Porcupines have no use for wood after its bark has been eaten, but most beavers do. Some pieces are used to mend old houses or to build new ones. Other pieces are added to dams which the animals build across streams. The dams hold back ponds in which the beavers swim, hide food logs, and build their dome-shaped houses.

# TREES AND LUMBER

BURR-RR, burr-rr! went a saw as it cut into a Douglas fir. Soon the men who were using the saw stopped to drive wedges into the cut. The wedges were pieces of wood made thin at one end and thick at the other. They kept the tree trunk from pressing down on the saw so hard that it could not move.

People who buy Douglas fir lumber sometimes call it "Oregon pine." Actually, the trees are neither pines nor firs, but are related to hemlocks. We can tell Douglas firs by their small cones, which have three-pointed parts called *bracts* extending beyond the scales. The needles are soft and flat, like those of hemlocks, and they never grow in clusters. The gray-brown bark of young trees is thin and smooth. The bark on old trunks becomes very thick, with deep furrows and wide ridges.

Douglas firs range from Mexico into Canada and from eastern Colorado to the Pacific Coast. This special tree grew near the coast of Oregon, where clouds that came from the ocean often caused fog or turned into rain. When the tree was young, its branches grew down to the ground, but as it became taller and taller, the lower branches died and dropped off. They left the trunk straight and smooth to a height of 150 feet. It was just what lumbermen needed to make plywood or boards.

The men with the saw talked about that as they went back to their work. "She's a nice clean tree," one of them said. "Sure is!" the other answered. "Well, let's get her down!"

Deeper and deeper went the saw, till the tree cracked and started to fall. A notch that had been cut with axes made it tip away from the men, but they took no chances. Dragging their saw, they ran away and stood behind another big tree. They also shouted, "Tim-ber!" loudly, warning other workmen to stay away.

The Douglas fir toppled slowly at first but soon came down with a crash. Then the men took saws and axes and trimmed

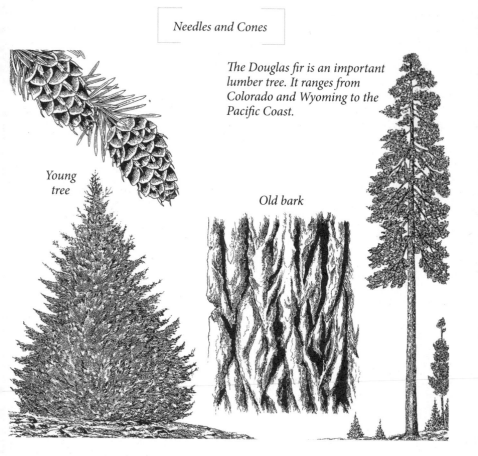

*Needles and Cones*

*The Douglas fir is an important lumber tree. It ranges from Colorado and Wyoming to the Pacific Coast.*

*Young tree*

*Old bark*

branches from the trunk. When that was done, the trunk was cut into several sections, called sawlogs. This was done because the whole trunk was too long to be moved.

There was a time when loggers cut, or felled, trees by hand and hauled them to rivers or railroads with horses. The logs then floated downstream to sawmills or were taken to them by trains.

Many logs are still carried by trains, some of which run on railroads owned by lumber companies. But horses are almost never used, especially to haul huge sawlogs like those cut from Douglas firs. Caterpillar tractors drag such logs to places where they can be loaded onto trucks. The trucks, which are big and powerful, then haul the logs to sawmills.

Douglas fir is one of the most important lumber trees in the United States. The wood is yellowish or pale brownish red, with a straight grain and very few knots. The wood also is strong and "works" well with hand tools or machinery. Douglas fir is sawed into boards and thicker lumber, and it is peeled into sheets which are glued, or bonded, together to make plywood. Branches and small pieces left over in sawmills are chopped up or ground to bits and then are made into paper. Douglas fir makes fine paper for writing and for books, as well as for bags, wrapping paper, and cardboard.

Many trees beside Douglas fir are cut and sawed into lumber. If you watch new houses go up, you are sure to see pinewood as well as spruce, fir, and probably cedar. You may find redwood, too, for it makes fine boards for siding, as well as thicker timbers. Oak and walnut are common in furniture, though some of the wood that is called walnut really comes from sweet gum trees. Most gymnasiums have floors of maple, and birch may be found in anything from spools to peach baskets.

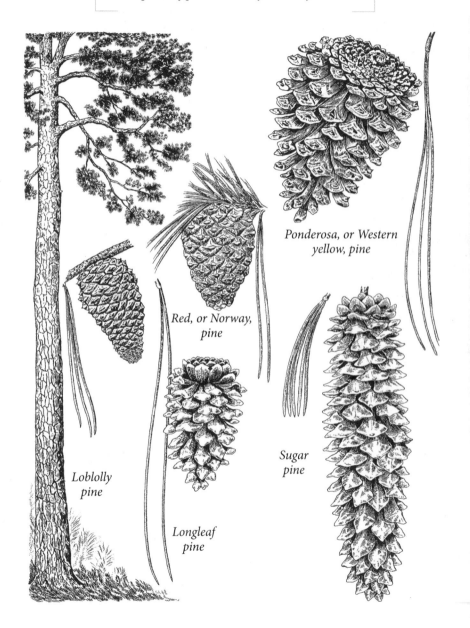

Some species of pine that are often used for lumber

Ponderosa, or Western yellow, pine

Red, or Norway, pine

Loblolly pine

Longleaf pine

Sugar pine

*Black walnut*

*Tulip tree*

*Swamp red oak*

*Three broad-leafed trees that are cut for lumber*

Trees that are not needed for lumber may be cut into pulpwood. Most pulpwood is made into paper, but part of it becomes cardboard, wallboard, cellophane, plastics, rayon, and films for photography. Douglas fir is an important Western pulpwood, and so is western hemlock. Spruce, firs, and pines are common pulpwoods in the East from Canada to Florida. Aspens and birches are cut for pulpwood, too, especially in the East.

Woods used for furniture are chosen partly for their color and hardness but mostly for their grain. Grain is the pattern of stripes, lines, and dashes that show when wood is "finished." Some of these markings are made by annual rings, which look quite different when wood is cut in different ways. Grain is also made by wood rays, which are sheets of short but very wide cells in which the trees store extra food. You can see these rays in many old weathered stumps. You can also see them, cut slant-wise, in "quarter-sawed" oak.

Large sap tubes show plainly in some kinds of wood, but most grain is made by wood fibers. Straight-grained, or even-grained, wood has fibers that run up and down. In many trees, however, the fibers bend this way and that way, or even twist. Wood from these trees has wavy, curly, or spiral grain.

Knots are the "stub" ends of small branches, surrounded by ordinary wood. The knots in most conifers are filled with rosin, a waste material. It keeps fungi from growing through dead stubs, and it gives the knots a rich brown color. Some knots shrink and split or fall out, leaving holes or making boards so weak that they break. Other knots fit so tightly that they form part of the wood. Many people use knotty pine boards on the walls of dining rooms and dens, or in cabinets.

*Some trees that are cut for pulpwood*

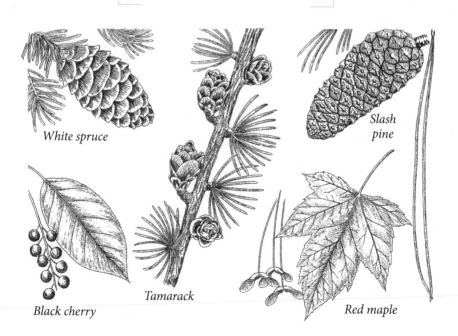

*White spruce*

*Slash pine*

*Black cherry*

*Tamarack*

*Red maple*

When white men first came to America, forests covered a large part of the country. Men had to cut trees down and burn them in order to clear land for farms.

As years went by, more trees were cut down and destroyed or sawed into lumber. Forest fires killed many trees, too, and so did diseases and insects. By 1918, trees were being used or killed about five times as fast as they were growing. If that kept on, America would soon run out of wood!

Then conditions began to change. People still used a great deal of wood and cut down millions of trees every year. But lumbermen learned to cut for *sustained yield*, which means that they took large, "ripe" trees and left the others to grow. People also tried to prevent forest fires and worked to keep insects and diseases from killing great numbers of trees. Millions of seedlings also were planted to grow where forests had been cut down or destroyed by fire.

All this took careful planning and hard work, but it has been successful. By 1955, American forests were growing as fast as they were used or killed by fires, diseases, and insects. The next step is to make forests grow a little faster. When they do so, we need not fear that we will ever run out of wood.

**THE END**